The

GW00384862

OZ isms

a tourist's guide & a giggle

Australian 'fun' etic slangwich

it's not wat ya say it's 'ow ya say it...

created for a laugh
by Melanie & Bo

Sagamore

Published by Sagamore Pty Ltd
ACN 001 534 989
P.O. Box 186, Gordon, New South Wales, 2072, Australia
www.sagamorebooks.com.au
email: publisher@sagamorebooks.com.au

Production Manager: Katie Jenkins
Illustrations, Text & Design layout
Copyright © Melanie & Roque 'Bo' Ablan III, 2011

First Published 2005
Revised Edition Published 2011

ISBN: 978-1-921913-02-0
Printed in China

Special ta to Lynnie, Ma, Dad,
Ginny & the Duke.

OZ-isms
BEFOREward

"g'day mate"

Youz all know what that means, right..?
So why, ya reckon, do youz need this
little black book..?

Aussies speak English.. don't they?
bloody oath!.. but hang on a tick, no one's
gunna tell ya you'll need a translator...!

So, if you wanna sound like a 'tru blu
dinki di Ocka' (that's a real **Aussie** to you) &
for the 'silly buggas' (the clowns among us)
who wanna 'av a good old 'cackle' (laugh)
or just for those of you who want a
'deadset rippa' (absolutely fabulous) little
souvenir to take home with ya.....

This one's for you!

Go on, get into it & give it a go u mug!!

CONTENTS

Dictionary of 'fun'etic WORDS

in alphabetical order

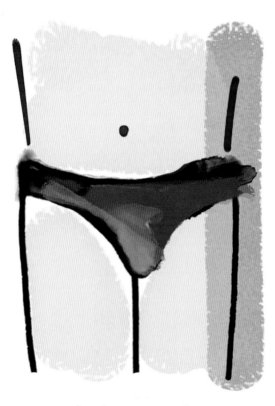

budgie smugglas
speedos, mens swim suit

OZ·isms Dictionary of '*fun*'etic WORDS

a looka	good looking
agog	astounded
aggro	aggressive
akubra	Aussie farm hat
alsoran	a nobody
amber liquid	beer
ankle biter	young child
anzac	WW1 soldier, a biscuit
apples	o.k, alright
arsehole	despicable person
arse licker	over pleaser
arvo	afternoon
Aunty	ABC TV
aussie salute	shooing flies away
average	ordinary
ay	a word used at the end of a sentence

back blocks	outer suburbs
backchat	talk back to
bad trot	not going well
baggy green	Aussie cricket cap
bail out	leave quickly, to help someone out
bail up	hold captive
balls up	mess up
bang on	that's right
bangers	sausages
barbie	barbecue
bar flies	pub regulars
barney	fight, argument
barrack	cheer your team
battler	has it tough
battleaxe	cranky old woman
beanie	knitted hat

OZ-isms Dictionary of 'fun'etic WORDS

beer belly	big stomach
beer o'clock	time to drink
belt up	be quiet
belly ache	complain
benchwarmer	a reserve in sport
bewdy	good, great
bickees	cookies
biddy	old lady
biff, biffo	punch up in footy
big ask	huge favour
big noter	person who brags
big smoke	the city
big spit	throw up, vomit
billabong	a waterhole
billy	tea, tea can
bingle	minor car accident
bite	react to something

bloke	man
bloodly oath	for sure
blunnies	leather work boots
bobydazzler	excellent
bomb	old car
Bondi cigar	turd in the water
bonk	have sex
bonkas	crazy
bonza	great
boofhead	stupid person
booze	alcohol
booze bus	police breath test
booze up	drink a lot
bottler	fantastic
bottlo	pub, liquor shop
bowser	gas pump
boxseat	best position

OZ-isms Dictionary of 'fun'etic WORDS

brass	money owners
brass razoo	worthless item
breakers	waves in the surf
brecky	breakfast
brewhaha	commotion
bricky	bricklayer
brickie's cleavage	bum crack
Brizzi	Brisbane
brollie	umbrella
bubbler	drinking fountain
budgie smugglas	speedos
bugger	damn
bugalugs	what's his name?
bull, bullshit	lie
bush telly	stars in the sky
bush tucker	native food
buster	man & South wind

blunnies
leather work boots

OZ·isms Dictionary of 'fun'etic WORDS

c'mon	come on
cab sav	red wine
cackla, cackle	giggler, laugh
cactus	ruined
cake face	makeup too heavy
cackie handed	left handed
cane	beat in a game
canoodle	cuddling
cark it	die
cashed up	have money
chalkie	school teacher
champas	champagne
chardy	chardonnay
checkout chick	cash register girl
chewie	chewing gum
cheesed off	annoyed
cheezee	too sweet
cherrie rype	choc & cherry bar

chicken	coward
chicken scratch	bad writing
chinwag	talk
chippie	carpenter
chips	french fries
chocka	full
choke one	take a shit
choof off	leave
choofers	smokers
chook	chicken
choppa	helicopter
choppers	false teeth
choyce	perfect
chuck in	give up
chuck up	to be sick, vomit
chunda	throw up
chundarous	revolting

OZ-isms Dictionary of *fun*'etic WORDS

clacka	the bottom
clobber	hit, punch, clothes
clod hoppers	big shoes
clot	idiot
clout	influence, hit
clucky	maternal
clued-up	well informed
cluey	clever
cobber	friend
cockie	cockatoo
cocky	arrogant
coldie	can of beer
cooee	call out
coot	difficult person
corka	really good
cow cocky	farmer
cracker	fireworks, great

chips
french fries

OZ·isms Dictionary of 'fun'etic WORDS

crack it	succeed in
cranky	grumpy
crawler	be overly nice to
creep	nasty person
crikey	oh my god
crim	a criminal
croc	a crocodile
crocodile skin	bad sun damage
crook	sick, a criminal
cross	angry
crusty	peeling
cozzie	swimsuit
cuppa	cup of tea
cushy	easy, good
cut	angry

dacks	trousers
dag	scruffy, untidy
daggy	unstylish person
damper	campfire bread
darl	darling
deadset	really
deadshit	a jerk
deep pockets	has lots of money
demo	demonstrate
derro	street person
devo'd	devastated
dickhead	fool
diddled	conned
digger	old man, soldier
dill	silly
dilly dally	waste time
ding	minor car damage

OZ·isms Dictionary of 'fun'etic WORDS

dingaling	silly person
dingbat	kooky person
dingy	dirty
dinky di	100% Australian
dip	swim
dobba	an informer
dob in	inform on
doco	documentary
domestic	couple's argument
dodgy	suspicious
dong	hit & penis
donga	penis
doodad	when you forget the word
doonybrook	fist fight
Down Under	Australia
droopy drawers	sluggish person

drongo	a fool
dropsies	dropping everything
drover	cattle or sheep person
dry up	be quiet
duds	trousers
dud	failure, doesn't work
duffer	silly person
dumper	big surf wave that knocks you over
dunno	don't know
dunny	toilet
dunlop overcoat	condom
duvalackie	something you forgot the name of

OZ·isms Dictionary of 'fun'etic WORDS

ear bash	lecture
ear basher	talks a lot
ear wigger	eaves dropper, listens in on
easy wicket	cushy job
egg on	encourage
egg beater	helicopter
elbow grease	manual labour, work at it
el cheapo	cheap
enzed	New Zealand
esky	food or drink cooler
even steven	equal

face fungus	beard, moustache
fag hag	female who hangs around homosexuals
fags	cigarettes, homosexuals
far gone	over the edge
fair cop	just result
fair dinkum	honest, for real
fair enough	o.k
fair go	fair treatment
fanny	vagina, bottom
fart arse	waste time
fat cats	wealthy people
fella	guy
feral	wild type
fess up	confess to
filthy	angry with

fizza	doesn't come up to expectations
fizzle out	disappointing end
fizzy	soft drink
fix	arrange, illegal
flabbergasted	stunned
flake out	collapse
flaming	same as 'bloody'
flannie, flanno	flannelette shirt
flat chat	busy
flat out	busy
flicks	movies
flip	stupid idiot
floater	turd in the toilet
flog	sell
fluff	fart
flutta	small bet

footy
football

OZ·isms Dictionary of 'fun'etic WORDS

footy	football
fossick	dig around
fox	hot chick
franga, frenchie	condom
freckles	chocolate candy
freebie	no charge
fridge	refrigerator
fried eggs	breasts
frisky	energetic
fruitloop	crazy, nutty
fuddy duddy	fussy
fu'gly	fucking ugly
full on	over the top, too much
fully sick	great
funny farm	psychiatric place
furphy	rumour

G & T	Gin & tonic drink
g ~ up	lift one's spirit
g ~ wizz	golly, goodness
ga ga	act silly over
gab	gossip
galah	silly person
galoot	foolish person
gander	look at
garbage guts	eats a lot
garbo	trash collector
gasbag	talk a lot, gossip
g'day	hello
geek	nerd
geeza	look at, old guy
gimmee	give me
gizmo	gadget
go'on	have a go, go on

OZ·isms Dictionary of 'fun'etic WORDS

gob	mouth
go crook	get angry
go dutch	pay your own way
got legs	credible, lasting
good oil	right information
good sort	attractive
googie	egg
gork at	stare, look at
goss	news, gossip
grass castle	house built from ill-gotten money
greaser	flatterer
grey suits	sharks
grog	alcohol
grog on	drink for hours
grommet	young surfer
grotty	dirty, grubby

grouse	great
grubby	untidy
grub	untidy person, food
grumblybum	complainer
gum puncher	dentist
gumboot	condom
gummy	shark
gunna	going to
gutless wonder	useless, coward
guzzla	takes a lot of fuel, alcoholic
gynormous	gigantic
gyp	cheat, dud

hairy eyeballs	angry look
half pinter	short person
hammie	hamstring muscle
handbag	attractive male companion
hang on	wait a minute
hard yakka	tough work
heaps	a lot
heart starter	early drink
heifers paddock	girls' school
hills hoist	clothes line
his nibs	the top dog, the boss
hit & giggle	tennis
home & hosed	sure thing
hoof it	by foot, walk
hooks	fingers
hooley dooley	holy smoke!

hills hoist
clothes line

OZ-isms Dictionary of 'fun'etic WORDS

hoon	reckless driver
hooter	nose
hostie	female flight crew
hottie	hot water bottle, sexy person
hot to trot	eager to go
hoyfaloy	upper class
hoytee toytee	snobby
hubby	husband
huey	weather God
humdinga	excellent
humpy	small shack
hunky dory	everything's good

iceberg	person who swims all year round
idiot box	television
iffy	doubtful, risky
in cactus	in trouble
intro	introduction
irish curtains	cobwebs
irish mist	light showers
iron out	fix a problem

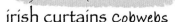

irish curtains cobwebs

jack	nothing
jackaroo	male trainee on a cattle station
jackass	idiot
jack-up	refuse to do
jamjars	thick lens glasses
jeggings	jean leggings
jiffy	short time
jiggered	broken
jillaroo	female trainee on a cattle station
joe blow	ordinary person
johnnycakes	damper, bread
journo	journalist
jug	kettle
jumbuck	sheep

k's	kilometres
kafuffle	commotion
kahoots	alliance
kaput	broken
kangaroo hop	jerky clutch release
keg party	beer barrel party
kelpie	aussie sheepdog
kero	kerosene
kick	wallet
kick in	start to work, contribute
kick on	continue
kiddiewinks	children
kindy	pre school
kingpin	head person
kip	nap

OZ·isms Dictionary of *'fun'etic* WORDS

kiteflier	person who writes a bouncing cheque
kiwi	New Zealander
kiwifruit	NZ fruit
kiwiland	New Zealand
knackered	very tired
knit pick	fussy, pick on
knock	criticise
knocka	person who criticises you
knockers	breasts
knock back	refuse, to consume quickly
knock off	finish work, to steal, a fake
knuckle sandwich	a punch in the mouth

lair	brash young man
lagger	police informer
lamington	Aussie cake
larrikin	mischievous youth
layabout	lazy person
legal eagles	lawyers
legless	drunk
legopeners	a drink, resulting in seduction
lemon	faulty, useless
let it rip	start up
lezzo	lesbian
lift	elevator
lickedysplit	quick smart
lip	back talk
lippie	lipstick

OZ·isms Dictionary of 'fun'etic WORDS

liquid lunch	to have only alcohol for lunch
loaded	drunk, drugged
lob up	arrive unexpected
local rag	local newspaper
local yokel	well known resident
lolly	candy
loo	toilet
looney bin	psychiatric place
lousy	no good
lout	hooligan
lurk	cushy
lush	a flirt, a heavy drinker

middy
small glass of beer

OZ·isms Dictionary of 'fun'etic WORDS

maggot	dirtbag
manbag	male handbag
mangle	destroy
mate	friend, unknown
mateship	camaraderie
mc mansion	suburban big house
mean	good, proficient
meggings	men's legging
merkin	female pubic hair
middy	small glass of beer
miffed	annoyed
milk bar	local store
mingy	stingy, little
missus	wife
mob	group of people
moll	loose female
molly-dooka	left handed

momance	men's friendship
mondayitis	Monday 'illness'
mongrel	mixed breed
monkey suit	dinner suit, tuxedo
moron	idiot
motza	lots of money
mozzie	mosquito
muck	mess
mudguard	vehicle fender
mug, muglair	vulgar male, showoff
muggy	humid
mullet	hair style
mulga	bush country
mushies	mushrooms
mystery bag	sausages

OZ·isms Dictionary of 'fun'etic WORDS

nada	nothing
nail	succeed, punish
nail bitter	exciting, close
nag, nagger	hassle, hassler
nanna	granny
nappy	diaper
narked	angry
natta	chatter
naughty	a word for sex
never never	outback country
nick	steal
nick off	leave, get lost
nightie	sleepwear
ningcompoop	dimwit
ninny	idiot
ningnong	stupid
nipper	junior lifesaver, kid

nippy	cold
nitty gritty	important part
nitwit	idiot
noah	shark
noggin	head
no hoper	loser
nong	fool
nookee	a word for sex
norks	breasts
norm	average
nosh	eat
not bad	very good
no worries	not a problem
nuddy	naked, nude
nucklehead	stupid
numbnuts	idiot

OZ-isms Dictionary of 'fun'etic WORDS

ocka	a real Aussie
ockerina	female Aussie
off load	get rid of, pass on
off sider	assistant
okee dokee	o.k, alright
old fella	penis
old hat	old fashioned
old man	father
oldies	parents
on spec	sight unseen
onya	good on you
oodles	lots
ooroo	good bye
or'rite	o.k
outback	remote country area
outlaws	in-laws
oy!	hey!

pluggers a.k.a thongs
backless rubber sandals

OZ·isms Dictionary of 'fun'etic WORDS

packing it	really scared
paddle pop	ice cream
paralytic	extremely drunk
pardon	excuse me
pash	kiss
pav	pavlova
peckish	mildly hungry
penguin	nun
penny pinching	watching your money
perks	extra benefits
perve	stare at lustfully
pesky	irritating, annoying
pigs	police
pig's arse	rubbish!
pig's bum	used in disbelief
pike, piker	give up easily
pinged	caught

piss	alcohol
pisshead	drinks a lot
pisspot	heavy drinker
pj's	pyjamas
plonk	cheap wine
pluggers	backless rubber sandals
pocket boxers	adjusting genitals
pokies	poker machines
pollie	politician
pollywaffles	chocolate candy
pom, pommy	Englishman
pong	smell, stink
poof, poofta	homosexual
pooped	tired
porky pie, porky	lie
postie	mail man

OZ·isms Dictionary of 'fun'etic WORDS

possum	dear
pozzy	your position
prang	car crash
prawn	weak person
preggers	pregnant
prezzie	gift
prop	hold up
psyched	excited
pub	hotel
punished	smashed
purla	heavy fall, really good
put in	do your best

plonk in a box
wine in a carton

OZ-isms Dictionary of 'fun'etic WORDS

quack	a doctor
queen	homosexual
queer	homosexual
quicksnort	fast drink
quid	money
quilt	blanket
quit	give up
quiver	surfboard collection

Quid money

rabbit on	talk nonsense
racehorse	thin rolled cigarette
rack off	get lost, go away
rag	newspaper
rags	menstruation
rapt	overjoyed
rashie	surfer's lycra vest
ratbag	rogue, rascal
ratshit, rs	no good, useless
ratty	shabby, bad temper
rattler	train
raw deal	unfair
raw prawn	try to fool you
razz	tease
reckie	check out a place
redhot	favourite
rego	car registration

OZ·isms Dictionary of *fun*'etic WORDS

rellies, rellos	your relatives
ridge didge	genuine, for real
rigmaroll	difficult procedure
ring in	substitute
rippa	terrific
rip off	cheat, defraud
ripsnorter	fabulous
ritee o	okay
roadie	last drink
rollie	roll your own
roll up	attendance
ron	later on
roo	kangaroo
root	a word for sex
rooted	exhausted
ropeable	very angry
rort	scheme

rorted	messed up, cheated
rotgut	cheap alcohol
rotten	angry, drunk
rough nut	unsophisticated
rough up	punch around
rouseabout	odd job man
rubber	eraser, condom
rubbaneck	sightseer
rubbish	trash, talk down
rugged	harsh
rugrats	small child, toddlers
run in	argument

OZ·isms Dictionary of 'fun'etic WORDS

same	agree with
sammie, sambo	sandwich
sandshoes	sneakers
sanger	sandwich, sausage
scab	nasty person
scads	lots
scallywag	mischievous person
scalper	ticket seller
schmick	stylish
schoolies	year 12 student's end of year celebration
schooner	large beer glass
schorcha	a really hot day
scone	head
scunge	untidy person
scungy	dirty
scratchie	instant lottery

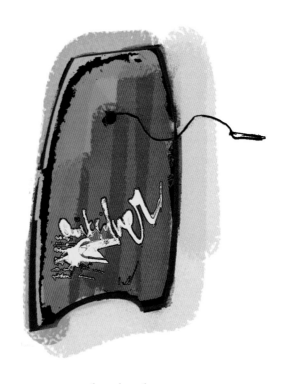

shark's biscuit
body board

OZ-isms Dictionary of 'fun'etic WORDS

screamer	spectacular
screw	have sex
screwed	no chance, had it
scribble	written notes
scrub	the bush
scrubba	rough woman
scumbag	lowlife person
search me	don't know
septic tank	yank, American
servo	gas station
settler's clock	kookaburra
shag	a word for sex
shaky isles	New Zealand
shank's pony	on foot
sharkbait	far out swimmer
shark's biscuit	body board
sheila	girl, chick

shemozzel	big mess
shellacking	badly defeated
shenanigans	get up to tricks
shickered	drunk
shiftee	suss
shilly shally	to & fro
shindig	party, event
shirty	angry, upset
shithouse	terrible, toilet
shocker	really bad
shonky	suspect, suspicious
shoo in	a sure win
short-arse	not a tall person
shout	buy the drinks
shove off	go away
shut eye	sleep
shrapnel	small change, coins

OZ·isms Dictionary of 'fun'etic WORDS

sick	cool, great
sickie	take a day off
silly season	Christmas
silvertail	upper class
simmer	calm down
sin bin	time out area
sinker	meat pie
skedaddle	go quickly
skew-wiff	askew
skerrick	small amount
skid lid	bicycle helmet
skite	brag, boastful
skittle	knock down
skull	drink in one go
sky pilot	clergyman
slack	lazy
slacka	lazy person

slag	cheap woman
slave-labour	hard work, bad pay
sloshed	drunk
slowcoach	slow
slug	inflict
smart alec	wiseguy
smashed	drunk, drugged up
smoko	take a short break
smooch	kiss
smoocha	kissing
smoodga	charmer
smooge	affectionate, cuddler
snaffle	steal
snag	sausage
snake's piss	cheap alcohol
snakey	irritable
snuff it	die

softcock	no courage
soft touch	a pushover
sook, sooky	cry-baby, wimpy
soup strainer	moustache
spagbol	spaghetti bolognaise
spare tyre	fat stomach
sparkie	electrician
sparrow's fart	dawn
spear off	leave
specky	spectacular
spineless	weak person
spittin'	light rain
speedo	speedometer, mens' swim suit
spew	to be sick
sponges	borrows
spook	spy

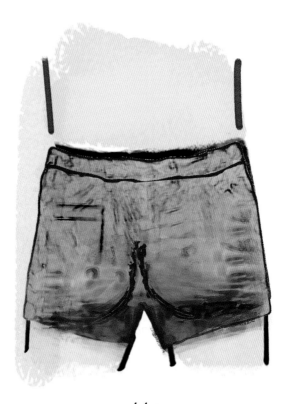

stubbies
men's shorts

OZ·isms Dictionary of 'fun'etic WORDS

sport	a person
spot on	correct, exactly
spray	criticise harshly
sprung	caught
square up	settle a debt
spud	potato
spruiker	shouting salesmen
spunk, spunky	sexy person, hot
squib	cowardly, mean
squiz	look at
stack	accident
staycation	vacation at home
stickybeek	busy body
stiff	too bad
stiffy	erection
stinjee	tight fisted
stink	fight

stinker	really hot day
stirra	creates friction
stoked	pleased
stoney broke	no money
stonkered	defeated, drunk
strapped	short of money
stoush	a brawl
streak, stretch	tall thin person
streaker	make a dash naked
strewth	goodness me
strides	trousers
stroppy	in a bad mood
stubby	short bottle of beer
stubbie	beer can cooler
stubbies	men's shorts
stuffed	exhausted, ruined
stuff up	mess up, mix up

OZ-isms Dictionary of 'fun'etic WORDS

suits	business men
sunnies	sunglasses
suppa	dinner
surf n turf	fish & meat meal
suss	suspicious
suss out	investigate
swag	sleeping bag
sweet	good
sweetie	nice person
sweetener	an incentive
swicheroo	exchange
swifty	a tricky act

ta	thanks
tacker	young child
tad	little
taddie	tadpole
tally	score, add up
tanked	drunk
tantie	tantrum
tattah	so long, goodbye
tatty	shabby
Tazzie	Tasmania
tea	dinner
tearjerker	movie that makes you cry
tee up	make arrangements
telly, TV	television
the box	television
the coathanger	Sydney Harbour Bridge

OZ·isms Dictionary of 'fun'etic WORDS

the goss	the news, gossip
the sticks	far country area
thingie, thingo	used if you don't
thingamejig	know the name
thingamebob	of something
thongs	rubber sandals
thunder box	outdoor toilet
thunder thighs	big legs
tick	a second
tick up	get credits
ticker	heart
tif	argument
tight arse	stingy
tinbum	to be lucky
tin ear	eavesdropper
tinker	naughty, to fiddle with

thunder box
outdoor toilet

OZ·isms Dictionary of 'fun'etic WORDS

tinny	can of beer
tit bits	information
tizzy	gaudy, worked up
toastie	toasted sandwich
toejam	dirty toenails
toey	bad tempered
togs	swimsuit
tonsil hockey	French kissing
toolies	out of school kids
toot	toilet
tommy	tomato sauce
tooshie	bottom
top	best, excellent
top drop	good wine
top end	Northern Territory
tubes	large cans of beer
trackies	tracksuit

U-ie	do a 'U' turn in a car
uggies	sheepskin boots
um	and
ump	umpire
unco	not coordinated
undies	panties, knickers
underdaks	underpants
under whelmed	not pleased
unit	big muscle man

uggies sheepskin boots

OZ·isms Dictionary of 'fun'etic WORDS

V-dub	volkswagon
vege {mite}	Aussie food spread
veggies	vegetables
veg out	do nothing
village bike	local hooker
vinnies	St Vincent de Paul, op shop
vino	wine
violet crumble	chocolate bar
voddies	vodka
volcanoes	pimples
vultures	lay in wait

Vege {mite}
Aussie food spread

OZ·isms Dictionary of 'fun'etic WORDS

wag	skip school
walkabout	go missing
wall flower	overlooked person
wallop	hit hard
walloper	policeman
wally	fool
wanka	idiot
waterworks	crying
watering hole	pub, hotel
wedding tackle	male genitals
weed	dope, tobacco
weekender	holiday house
weirdo	crazy person
wellies	gumboots
well heeled	wealthy
well oiled	drunk
welsh on	inform on, betray

Westies	from the Western suburbs
whack	hit
whacko	terrific
wharfie	dock worker
whatsa'name?	what's his/her name?
whatsit?	what's that thing?
whatchama'callit?	what do you call it?
whinger	complainer
whirl	give a go, try
white pointers	breasts
whippasnapper	young kid
whoopydo	who cares?
whoppa	enormous lie
whoozi whatsit	what's that thing?
willies	give you the creeps

OZ-isms Dictionary of 'fun'etic WORDS

willy nilly	any which way
willy willy	dust storm
wing nut	big ears
winner	fabulous, great
wonky	uneven
wowser	spoils the fun
woofa	dog
woopsidaisy	oops, be careful
woop woop	a remote place
worrywart	always worries
woose	coward
woosie	weak person
woozy	dizzy
wrapped	really pleased
wrinklie	old person
write off	unusable

yabba	talk alot
yabbie	crayfish
yack	talk
yakka	work
yahoo	loudmouth
Yank	an American
yarn	story
yawn	bore
yea	yes
yobbo	Aussie slob
yonks	a long time
yonnie	skimming stone
youngan'	kid, child
youz	you, all of you
yuck	
yucko	disgusting
yucky	

OZ-isms Dictionary of 'fun'etic WORDS

zack	sixpence
zeezz	nap
ziff	beard
zilch	nothing
zip	zero
zonked	passed out

zack sixpence

tinny in a stubbie
beer in a cooler cup

OZ·isms Dictionary of 'fun'etic WORDS

Dictionary of
'fun'etic
PHRASES
& EXPRESSIONS

in alphabetical order

a bit toey	impatient, off
a chip off the old block	like father, like son
a tall drink of water	a tall person
across the ditch	AKA New Zealand
act the goat	behave foolishly
a hit & a giggle	fun & games
all froth & no beer	all show & no substance
all laired up	dressed up
all piss n' wind	boastful, brag
all over d place	chaos
all show no blow	not as it seems
arse around	fool about
arse over tit	fall over
as bold as brass	confident, cocky
as right as rain	feeling great

as rough as guts	a poor job
as scarce as hen's teeth	rare, hard to find
arthur or martha	uncertain
at 6's & 7's	undecided
av a crack	to attempt
av a ganda	take a look
av a root	have sex
av a go	give it a try
av a good one	have a nice day
av a smokko	take a break at work
av a squiz at	have a look at
av you got rocks in ya head?	are you stupid?
av you lost ya marbles?	you crazy?
away with the pixies	daydreaming

back of Bourke	remote place
bald as a bandicoot	have no hair
bananabenda	Queenslander
bark's worse than your bite	all talk & no action
barkin' mad	really angry
bat outta hell	really fast
bee in ya bonnet	obsessed with
beetle crushers	boots
bend over backwards	try to please
big note ya self	praise yourself
bite the bullet	accept it
bite ya bum	shut up
bloody bastard	arsehole
bloody oath	you bet
blow a fuse	lose your temper

blow through	leave & don't pay
blow ya dough	spend your money
blow ya stack	lose your temper
bob's ya uncle	everything's fine
boil the billy	put the kettle on
brand spankin'	new
brick short of a load	simple minded
brown nose	flattery for gain
buck up	cheer up
buggered if I know	don't know
bull at a gate	obsessive, stubborn
bullamakanka	a far away place
bung it on	put on an act
bun in the oven	pregnant
by hook or by crook	do whatever it takes

by the skin of ur teeth
B.Y.O

just in time
bring your own alcohol

boil the billy
put the kettle on

call it quits	stop, give up
cashed up	lots of money
chalk & cheese	nothing alike
charge like a wounded bull	to have very high prices
cheap as chips	very inexpensive
chew the fat	have a chat
chew & spew	bad fast food
chip off d old block	someone who's just like their parents
chock a block	crowded, full
chuck a spaz	throw a tantrum
chuck a willy chuck a wobbly }	get hysterical
chuck a U-ie	do a 'U' turn
chuck in	contribute

chuck it in	give up
chuck out	throw away
come a cropper	fall hard
come off it	be reasonable
cop it sweet	got caught & take the blame
cotton on to	to understand
could eat a horse	starving
couldn't give a stuff	don't care
crack it hardy	put on a good face
crack me one	open a beer
crack the whip	put pressure on
cut me sum slack	give me a break
c ya later	good bye

dead as a door nail	ruined, no good, asleep
dead to the world	in a deep sleep
deliver the goods	do what you say
didn't bat an eye	no reaction
didn't come down in the last shower?	i'm not stupid
dirty on	angry with
divvy up	share the proceeds
do a runna	take off, leave
do ova	beat up
do the dirty	go behind your back
do ya block	lose your temper
do ya dash	reach the limit
do ya nana	have a tantrum
dog's breakfast	mess, untidy
doesn't give a bugger	couldn't care less

down the gurgla
down the drain

doesn't miss a trick	alert, sharp
done like a dog's dinner	defeated badly
don't come the raw prawn	don't try to fool me
don't count ya chickens before they hatch	pre-confident
don't give a rats ass	don't care
don't know ya from a bar of soap	a complete stranger
down in the dumps	unhappy
down the gurgla	down the drain
down the track	in the future
drag the chain	go too slowly, lag
drop a clanger	make a blunder
drop your guts	to fart

easy as	simple
easy as pushin' shit up hill	very, very difficult
easy wicket	easy job
el cheapo	cheap & nasty
esky	portable cooler
even steven	equal chance

esky portable cooler

fair crack of the whip	be reasonable
fair suck of the sav	be fair
fair dinkum	honest
fan-bloody-tastic	really great
fart around	waste time
fart arse around	mucking about
fed up to the back teeth	had enough
fell off the back of a truck	stolen
find a pozzie	get a position
flappin' ya gums	talking too much
flat as a tack	really flat
flat chat	very busy
flog the cat	pity oneself
fly d Aussie flag	shirt hanging out

fly off the handle	yell & scream at
folding stuff	paper money notes
for crying out loud	to be annoyed
for ron	keep for later
for starters	to begin with..
fossick around	look for something
frilled lizard	whiskered face
full as a boot	drunk
full as a goog	stuffed, full of food
full of beans	energetic
full of himself	conceited, thinks highly of himself
full of it	talking a load of nonsense
fuzzy wuzzy angels	Papua New Guinea natives who helped Aussie soldiers in WWII

garbage guts	person eating a lot
g'day sport	male greeting
get a guernsey	to be chosen
get a grip	get it together
get a handle on	to understand
get amongst it	have a go
get a wriggle on	hurry up
get into it	give it a go
get on with it	hurry up
get ova it	forget it
get nicked	get lost, go away
get off me back	stop nagging
get off me hamma	driving too close
get some shut eye	go to sleep
get stuffed	get lost
get stuck into it	start, dig in
get the arse	fired from a job

get the nod	given approval
get up ya nose	annoying
get ya arse into gear	get organised
give it a whirl	have a try
give it a rap	praise
give it away	stop, give up
give it the flick	throw out
glutton for punishment	difficult, unpleasant tasks
go crook on	be angry with
go bush	leave the city
go for ya life	give it your all
go like the clappers	go really fast
go off half cocked	go unprepared

go to buggery	go away
go troppo	go berserk
go walkabout	wander off
goes to the opening of an envelope	attend every function
good on the tooth	good appetite
got legs	credible
great Aussie salute	shoo flies away
grin & chronic	gin & tonic
gut renching	heart breaking
guttless wonda	wimp

hairy cheque book	old man who supports a young woman
half ya luck	to be fortunate
hammer & tongs	full on
hang on a tic	wait a minute
happy as Larry	really pleased
hard yakka	hard work
has a snout on	has a grudge
hasn't got a cracker	has no money
haul ya ova the coals	get stuck into
have a chardi	drink white wine
have a dig	criticise
have a lash	try, take part
have a slash	to urinate
have a snort	take a drink

have a sticky	look at, pry
have a tanty	throw a tantrum
have a vommi	be sick, throw up
have sum champas	drink champagne
havin' a blinda	having a good one, to get absolutely drunk
hell for leather	go flat out
hide nor hair	nowhere to be seen
hit the sack	go to bed
hook, line & sinka	everything, the lot
hump a bluey	carry a swag

hump a bluey
carry a swag

icing on the cake	added extra
I'll be a monkey's uncle	astounded
I'll be buggered	to be surprised
I'm easy	not fussed
I'm over it	that's enough
in a jiffy	in a second
in a tick	in a minute
in a tizz	angry, excited
in good nick	in good condition
in kahoots with	in alliance with
in like Flynn	well placed
in the bag	a sure thing
in the drink	in the water
in the nick	jail
in the nuddy	naked, nude
in the poo	in trouble

in the raw	naked
in two ticks	soon
in ya face	pushy
iron 'em out	punch, sort out
isn't worth a pinch of salt	useless
it'll be rite	it's o.k.
it'll be sweet	it's fine
it'll keep	it can wait
it's a hair past a freckle	the time when not wearing a watch
it's a goer	go ahead with
it's pissin' down	raining heavily
it's the pits	the worst
i've seen a better head on a glass of beer	they're ugly

jack in the box	someone who can't sit still
jack of that	fed up or tired of doing something
jolly green giant	Aussie $100 note
just down the road	close by, can also mean far away
just joshing ya	only kidding

keen as mustard	very eager
keep it on the lolo	low profile
keep ur mitts off	don't touch
keg on legs	one who drinks a lot
kick in the teeth	slap in the face
kick the bucket	die
kick up the arse	pull into line
kick up a stink	make a big fuss
kit & kaboodel	the lot
knock it off	stop it
knock on the head	put an end to
knock ya block off	hit on the head
knock yaself out	go ahead, allow
know a thing or two	to be wise

lay doggo	pretending, still
leak like a sieve	can't keep secrets
left for dead	abandoned
let sleepin' dogs lie	leave it be
let ur head go	splurge
lift ya game	to improve
like a blue arsed fly	frantic
like a shag on a rock	left, alone
like a stunned mullet	bewildered
like a two bob watch	erratic manner, useless
like death warmed up	look sick
lights on, no one home	unintelligent

living the life of
  Riley   the good life
lock, stock &
  barrel   everything
look at moi   look at me
looks like an
  unmade bed   untidy
lull about   laze around

mad as a cut snake   crazy

make a mug of
     ya self   embarrass yourself

make a quid   earn a living

make tracks   get going

mate's rates   at a reduced price

me ute   my utility vehicle

me ol' lady   my mother

me ol' man   my father

more arse than
     class   more luck than skill

muck about   mess around

mutton dressed
     as lamb   dressing too young
         for your age

me ute
utility vehicle

nasty piece of work	not a nice person
no skin off my nose	doesn't worry me
nose down, bum up	to be very busy
not a brass razoo	broke, no money
not a patch on	not as good as
not for quids	no chance
not fussed	not worried
not on your nellie	no way
not the full quid	unintelligent
not worth a bar of soap	useless
not worth a cracka	worthless
nothin' out of the box	ordinary
nothin' to write home about	nothing special
now ur cookin'	get the hang of it

off the beaten track	gone bush
off like a bride's nightie	leave fast
off with the pixies	daydreaming
off ya face	really out of it
off ya tucka	lost your appetite
on a good wicket	doing well
on a sticky wicket	in trouble
on the ball	sharp, attentive
on the blink	not working
on the nose	smelly, suspect
on the rag	menstruating
on the turps	heavy drinker
on ya bike	get going
'on ya mate	good on you
one fer ron	take for later

open slather	open opportunity
open the flood gates	let it all go
order of the boot	fired
out for lunch	no concentration
out like a light	get knocked out, fall asleep quickly
out of the box	special
out of the loop	on the outside
out of whack	not aligned
out to grass	retire
over the moon	ecstatic
ow much izit?	what's the cost?
'ow ya goin'?	how are you?

packapoo ticket	untidy
pack a wallop	hit hard
packin' death	really scared
packin' it	very scared
pack it in	give up
pain in ya pinnie	stomach ache
park ya bum	sit down
pay through the nose	pay too much
pick ya brains	ask questions
piece of cake	easy
pillow rider	homosexual
polish off	finish
piss in the wind	ineffective
piss off	go away
playin' possum	pretending
pull a swifty	trick

pull the pin	get out
pull up stumps	leave
pull ur finger out	get on with it
pull ur head in	back off, shut up
pull ya socks up	improve
put a cork in it	shut up
put in the hard yards	to work hard
put the billy on	make a cup of tea
put the boot in	attack when one is already down
put the bite on	ask for money
put the hard word on	proposition
put up or shut up	do something or keep quiet
put up ya dooks	a fight challenge

rattle ya dags	get a move on
right as rain	okay
rip or bust	no matter what
rough as guts	uncouth, thug
rough end of the pineapple	be on the bad side of the deal
rough head	ugly
rouse on	shout at
rub it in	make you feel worse
rub ya nose in it	won't let you forget
run amuck	go wild
run around like a chook with its head cut off	confused state
run of outs	losing streak
run out of legs	exhausted
rush ya fences	act too quickly

say when	you have enough?
shaggin' wagon	panel van
sharp as a cut snake	wise, smart
she'll be apples	everything is fine
she'll be right	it'll be fine
she'll be sweet	it'll be good
shoot thru	run away
shot full of holes	put down, drunk
show you the ropes	teach you how
side kick	a junior
silly as a 2 bob watch	stupid
silly buggas	acting stupid
sink a few	have a beer or two
snag sanga	sausage sandwich

snag sanga
sausage sandwich

snug as a bug in a rug	cosy
soft peddling	going slow
southerly busta	strong south wind
spanner in the works	an obstacle
spill the beans	divulge a secret
spittin' chips	furious
spit the dummy	throw a tantrum
sponge off	freeload
standover merchant	a bully
stands out like dog's balls	obvious
stick the boot in	kick you when you're down
stoked as	really pleased, happy
stone the crows	unbelievable

strapped for cash	short of money
strike a blow	start work
strike me lucky	pleasant surprise
strike me pink	can't believe it
stuffed up	made a mistake
stunned mullet	look of surprise
swaning about	showing off
sweat it out	wait patiently
sweet as	perfect
sumthing or other	used when you don't know the word for the thing

take a load off	sit down
take a piece of	tell off
take a punt	take a chance
take a pew	sit down
take a shine to	to like someone
take a sickie	take the day off
take a squiz	have a look
take it with a grain of salt	deal with it, don't care
take the mickey	send up, tease
take the piss	make fun of
take ya to the cleaners	take all your money
tail between ya legs	embarrassed, beaten
talk ya blind	won't stop talking
tear strips off ya	give you a hard time
tell 'im is dreamin'	got no chance

that's a bit rich	that's harsh
thick as a brick	not too smart
that's a snack	easy
the writing's on the wall	all the signs are there
think the sun shines out of ya arse	love yourself
throw a tanty	have a tantrum
throw in the towel	give up
tickets onya self	to be stuck up
tickle the ivories	play the piano
tickle the till	rob, embezzle
tight as a fish's arse	stingy
tinny in a stubbie	beer in a cooler cup
tip of the iceberg	just the beginning
tit for tat	pay back in kind

to be a fly on the wall	watch unseen
to do the dirty	go behind your back
to leave a bad taste	not as expected
tongue in cheek	sarcastic
too rite mate	that's correct
tore into me	had a go at me
tore strips off me	verbally attack
tough titty	too bad
try it on	deceive
tuck into it	start eating
turn it up	get real
turn it on	over do it, flatter
twig on to	understand
two bites of the cherry	two chances

two bob each way	sit on the fence
two bob lair	cheap flashy male
two bob short of a quid	not all there
two men & a dog	poor attendance
two pot screamer	easy drunk
two shakes of a lamb's tail	just a second

up his alley	suits the person
up the duff	to be pregnant
up the pole	confused
up shit creek without a paddle	in big trouble
up yours	up your bum

vatican roulette	rhythm method of contraception
verandah above the toyshop	a male paunch, a big stomach
vickta	lawn mower
village bike	local prostitute
Vinnies special	op shop purchase
vote with ya feet	walk away

vickta
lawn mower

wake up to ya self	be sensible
walking papers	get fired
water off a duck's back	it doesn't bother you, not affected
weak as cats' piss	weak drink
were ya born ina tent?	said when the door is left open
wet the whistle	have a drink
what a hoot	what a laugh
what a rippa	that's fabulous
what are ya	sarcastic exclaim
what d'ya think this is	said in disgust
what's the damage?	what do I owe you
what's the go	what's happening

what's the game	what are you up to
what d'ya do for a crust?	what is your profession ?
what's ya beef?	what's the problem
when the shit hits the fan	when something gets exposed
whole shebang	everything
with a fine tooth comb	meticulously
within cooee	close enough
won't have a bar of it	take no part in it
would knock ya socks off	amazing

wouldn't be dead
for quids   *loving life*

wouldn't give ya the
time of day   *un-cooperative*

wouldn't know his arse
from his elbow   *idiot, stupid*

wouldn't miss it for
quids   *could not keep
me away*

wouldn't touch it with
a 40 foot pole   *have nothing to
do with*

ya game?	you brave enough?
ya not wrong	you're right
ya cotton on? ya know what i mean?	do you understand
ya reckon?	do you think so?
ya right	you're welcome
ya off ya nana	you're crazy
ya wouldn't read about it	unexpected
you bloody bewdy	that's great
you little bewdy	fantastic
you little ripper	fantastic
you nailed it	you did it
you pullin' me leg?	are you joking?
you shithead	you idiot
you up for it?	are you ready?

you're a legend	you're great
you're a dead duck	in big trouble
you're a tool	you're an idiot
you're bullshittin'	you're lying
you're the limit	you're impossible
you're up yourself	big headed, big ego
you've got a be in it to win it	you've got to have a go
you've got buckleys	not a chance, no way
you've got a screw loose	you're crazy
youz all	everyone

Scribble page
for ya own **OZ**-isms
in case I've missed a few

_____

_____

_____

_____

_____

_____

_____

_____

_____

_____

_____

_____

_____

_____

OZ-isms
AFTERward

Could gab on bout the hard yakka put into this, but i'd be tellin' ya a porky-pie.

So i'll give it to ya fair dinkum...

All these bloody whatchamacallits.. **OZ**-isms, came from me mates & rellos & every Joe Blow, sheila & bloke i ever met in our land Down Under..

So Ta to all you ockas across this big brown land of Oz..!

You'z all know who you'z r...sweet!

c ya ...

ps. Oh yeah, s'pose i don't áv t tell ya dis ain't d proper English spelling... its d **OZ**-isms way of spelling!